# INTERMEDIATE SET #2

## RUDIMENTS EXAM SERIES

By Glory St. Germain ARCT RMT MYCC UMTC
Shelagh McKibbon-U'Ren RMT UMTC

# GSG MUSIC

*Enriching Lives Through Music Education*

ISBN: 978-1-927641-05-7

# The Ultimate Music Theory™ Program
*Enriching Lives Through Music Education*

The Ultimate Music Theory™ Workbooks & Answer Books Program includes:

**UMT Rudiments Workbooks** for Prep 1, Prep 2, Basic, Intermediate, Advanced & Complete
**UMT Exam Series** (Set #1 & Set #2) for Preparatory, Basic, Intermediate & Advanced

**Supplemental Workbooks** for PREP LEVEL, LEVELS 1 - 8 & COMPLETE LEVEL
**UMT Supplemental Exam Series** for LEVEL 5, LEVEL 6, LEVEL 7 & LEVEL 8

The Ultimate Music Theory Program is the *Way to Score Success* as UMT helps students prepare for nationally recognized theory examinations including the Royal Conservatory of Music.

 Library and Archives Canada Cataloguing in Publication. UMT Workbooks & Exam Series /Glory St. Germain & Shelagh McKibbon-U'Ren. Respect Copyright. All rights reserved. GlorylandPublishing.com

**Ultimate Music Theory Rudiments Exam Series**

| | | |
|---|---|---|
| GP - EPS1 | ISBN: 978-1-927641-00-2 | Preparatory Rudiments Exams Set #1 |
| GP - EPS1A | ISBN: 978-1-927641-08-8 | Preparatory Exams Answers Set #1 |
| GP - EPS2 | ISBN: 978-1-927641-01-9 | Preparatory Rudiments Exams Set #2 |
| GP - EPS2A | ISBN: 978-1-927641-09-5 | Preparatory Exams Answers Set #2 |
| GP - EBS1 | ISBN: 978-1-927641-02-6 | Basic Rudiments Exams Set #1 |
| GP - EBS1A | ISBN: 978-1-927641-10-1 | Basic Exams Answers Set #1 |
| GP - EBS2 | ISBN: 978-1-927641-03-3 | Basic Rudiments Exams Set #2 |
| GP - EBS2A | ISBN: 978-1-927641-11-8 | Basic Exams Answers Set #2 |
| GP - EIS1 | ISBN: 978-1-927641-04-0 | Intermediate Rudiments Exams Set #1 |
| GP - EIS1A | ISBN: 978-1-927641-12-5 | Intermediate Exams Answers Set #1 |
| GP - EIS2 | ISBN: 978-1-927641-05-7 | Intermediate Rudiments Exams Set #2 |
| GP - EIS2A | ISBN: 978-1-927641-13-2 | Intermediate Exams Answers Set #2 |
| GP - EAS1 | ISBN: 978-1-927641-06-4 | Advanced Rudiments Exams Set #1 |
| GP - EAS1A | ISBN: 978-1-927641-14-9 | Advanced Exams Answers Set #1 |
| GP - EAS2 | ISBN: 978-1-927641-07-1 | Advanced Rudiments Exams Set #2 |
| GP - EAS2A | ISBN: 978-1-927641-15-6 | Advanced Exams Answers Set #2 |

**Ultimate Music Theory Supplemental Exam Series**

| | | |
|---|---|---|
| GP-L5E | ISBN: 978-1-990358-11-1 | LEVEL 5 Exams |
| GP-L5EA | ISBN: 978-1-990358-12-8 | LEVEL 5 Exams Answers |
| GP-L6E | ISBN: 978-1-990358-13-5 | LEVEL 6 Exams |
| GP-L6EA | ISBN: 978-1-990358-14-2 | LEVEL 6 Exams Answers |
| GP-L7E | ISBN: 978-1-990358-15-9 | LEVEL 7 Exams |
| GP-L7EA | ISBN: 978-1-990358-16-6 | LEVEL 7 Exams Answers |
| GP-L8E | ISBN: 978-1-990358-17-3 | LEVEL 8 Exams |
| GP-L8EA | ISBN: 978-1-990358-18-0 | LEVEL 8 Exams Answers |

Go to UltimateMusicTheory.com **and check out the FREE Resources**

Ultimate Music Theory FREE RESOURCES created just for you!

The **Ultimate Music Theory Exams** reinforce the **UMT Intermediate Rudiments Workbook** and prepare students for continued learning with UMT Advanced Rudiments.

**Intermediate Rudiments Theory Examination** requirements include Basic Rudiments requirements plus the following:

### Pitch
- Double sharps and double flats

### Rhythm
- Note and rest time values (breve, whole, half, quarter, eighth, sixteenth and thirty-second)
- Double dotted notes
- Time Signatures in Simple Time and in Compound Time
- Irregular groups in Simple Time (quintuplets and septuplets)

### Scales in Major and minor keys up to and including seven sharps and seven flats
- Write or identify: Major and minor (natural, harmonic and melodic) scales, ascending and descending
- Write or identify: Related keys: relative Major and minor, tonic (parallel) Major and minor; enharmonic Major and minor
- Write or identify: Technical degree names of the scale degrees
- Write or identify: Whole-tone scales and chromatic scales (using any standard version)
- Identify: blues scales, Major pentatonic scales, minor pentatonic scales and octatonic scales

### Triads in all Major and harmonic minor keys
- Write: Solid (blocked) in Root Position and inversions (close position only)
- Identify: Solid (blocked) or broken in Root Position and inversions (close position or open position)

### Intervals - Perfect, Major and minor
- Write or identify: above or below a given note, all intervals and their inversions up to and including an octave, melodic or harmonic form (with or without a Key Signature)

### Recognition of Key Signatures up to and including seven sharps and seven flats
- Identify the key (Major or minor) of a given melody with a Key Signature
- Rewrite the excerpt using the correct Key Signature and identify the key (Major or minor)

### Transposition (Major Keys up to and including seven sharps and seven flats)
- Transpose a melody up or down any interval within the octave

### Cadences in all Major and harmonic minor keys
- Identify cadences in keyboard style only in a musical excerpt
- Perfect (Authentic): V - I (Major) and V - i (minor); Plagal: IV - I (Major) and iv - i (minor); Imperfect (Half Cadence): I - V or IV - V (Major) and i - V or iv - V (minor)

### Musical Terms and Signs
- Recognize, define or supply the musical terms or signs as listed in the Intermediate Rudiments Workbook

### Analysis
- Analyze a short musical composition, identifying any of the above theory requirements

### Score:
   **60 - 69** Pass;   **70 - 79** Honors;   **80 - 89** First Class Honors;   **90 - 100** First Class Honors with Distinction

## Ultimate Music Theory: *The Way to Score Success!*

UltimateMusicTheory.com © Copyright 2013 Gloryland Publishing. All Rights Reserved.

# ULTIMATE MUSIC THEORY
## INTERMEDIATE EXAM SET #2 - EXAM #1

Total Score: ____
100

> ♪ **UMT Tip:** Before beginning your exam, write out the Circle of Fifths. Write the order of flats and sharps. Write the Major keys on the outside of the circle and the relative minor keys on the inside of the circle.

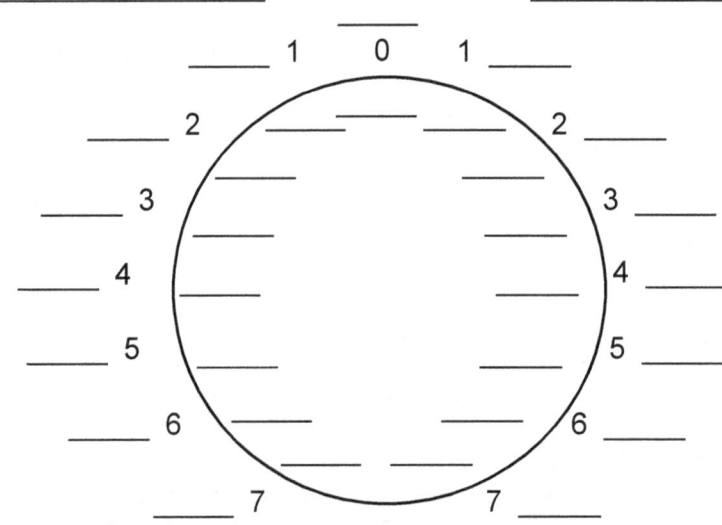

> ♪ **UMT Tip:** When writing an interval of a harmonic Aug 1, and both notes require accidentals, write the touching notes first. Then add BOTH accidentals in front of the touching notes. The lower accidental is always written first. (♭♮ or ♮♯ etc.)

1. a) Name the following harmonic intervals.

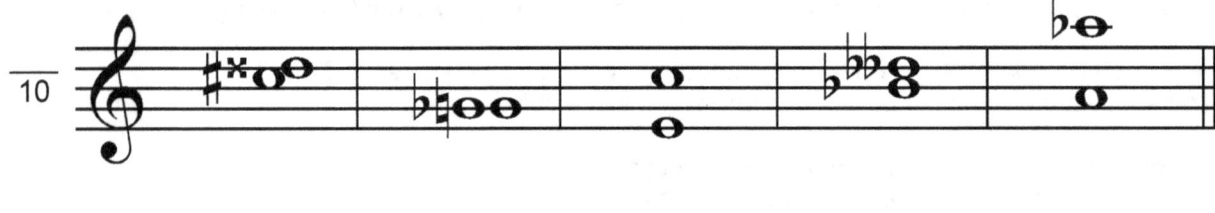

b) Invert the above harmonic intervals in the given clef. Name the inversions.

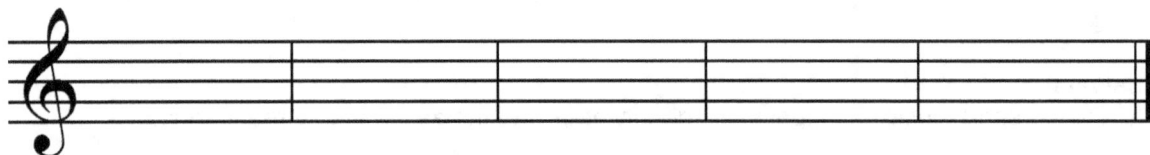

UltimateMusicTheory.com © Copyright 2013 Gloryland Publishing. All Rights Reserved.

# ULTIMATE MUSIC THEORY
## INTERMEDIATE EXAM SET #2 - EXAM #1

> ♪ **UMT Tip:** A triad in close position is written as close together as possible. No interval is larger than a 6th.

2. a) Write the following solid triads in close position in the Treble Clef. Use the correct Key Signature and any necessary accidentals. Use whole notes.

[10]

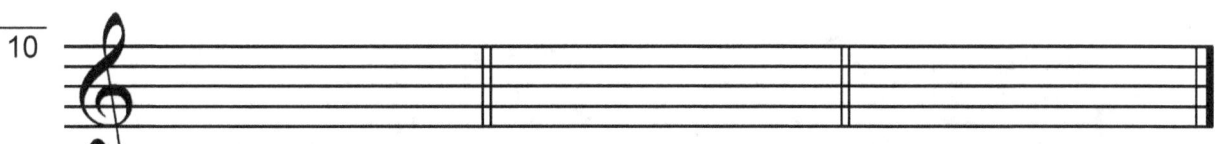

        Tonic triad of        Submediant triad of        Dominant triad of
        b minor harmonic        B Major        D flat Major
        in second inversion        in root position        in first inversion

b) Write the following solid triads in close position in the Bass Clef. Use accidentals. Use whole notes.

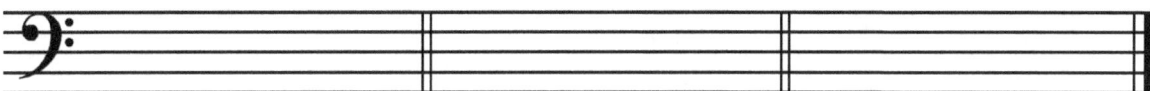

        Mediant triad of        Submediant triad of        Subdominant triad of
        F Major        d minor harmonic        C sharp Major
        in first inversion        in second inversion        in root position

> ♪ **UMT Tip:** A triad in open position is written with intervals that can be larger than a 6th. One of the notes (usually the Root) may be doubled.

c) Identify the root note and the quality/type of each of the following open position triads.

Root Note: _____  _____  _____  _____

Quality/Type: _____  _____  _____  _____

UltimateMusicTheory.com © Copyright 2013 Gloryland Publishing. All Rights Reserved.

# ULTIMATE MUSIC THEORY
## INTERMEDIATE EXAM SET #2 - EXAM #1

♪ **UMT Tip:** Rewrite the bar lines first before transposing the notes.

3. The following melody is in the key of B Major.
   a) Transpose the given melody UP a diminished fifth. Use the correct Key Signature.
   b) Name the key of the new melody.

Key: B Major

Key: _____

♪ **UMT Tip:** Name the accidentals in order of the Key Signature. A melodic fragment may not contain all the accidentals in the key.

The following melody has been written using accidentals instead of a Key Signature.
c) Name the key of the given melody.
d) Rewrite the given melody using the correct Key Signature and any necessary accidentals.

Key: _____

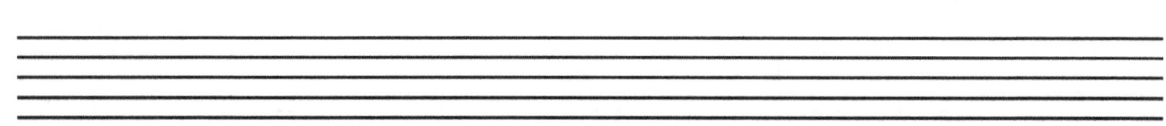

UltimateMusicTheory.com © Copyright 2013 Gloryland Publishing. All Rights Reserved.

# ULTIMATE MUSIC THEORY
## INTERMEDIATE EXAM SET #2 - EXAM #1

> ♪ **UMT Tip:** Count the number of notes and identify the pattern of tones and semitones.

4. Name the following scales as Major, natural minor, harmonic minor, melodic minor, blues, Major pentatonic, minor pentatonic, octatonic, chromatic or whole tone.

10

a) _____

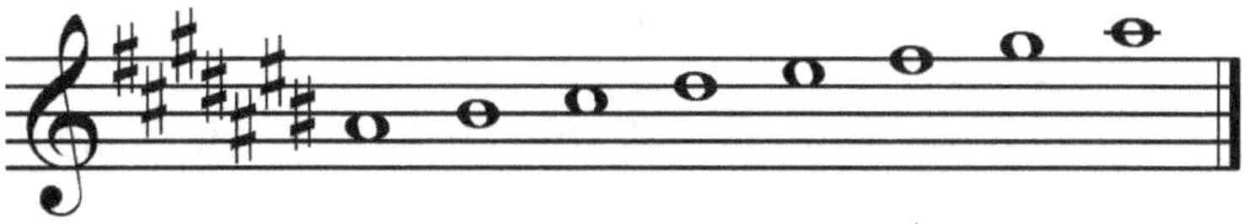

b) _____

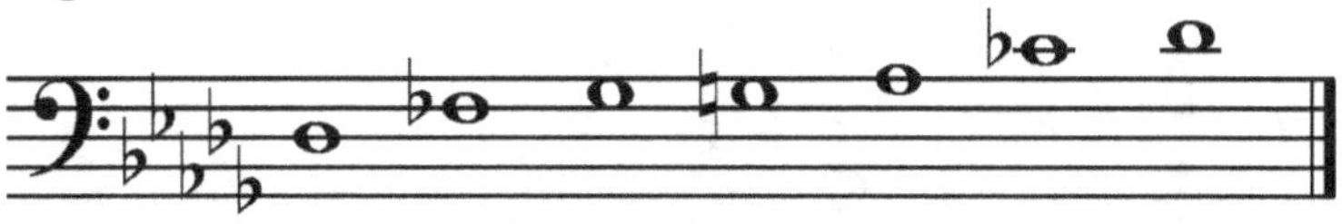

c) _____

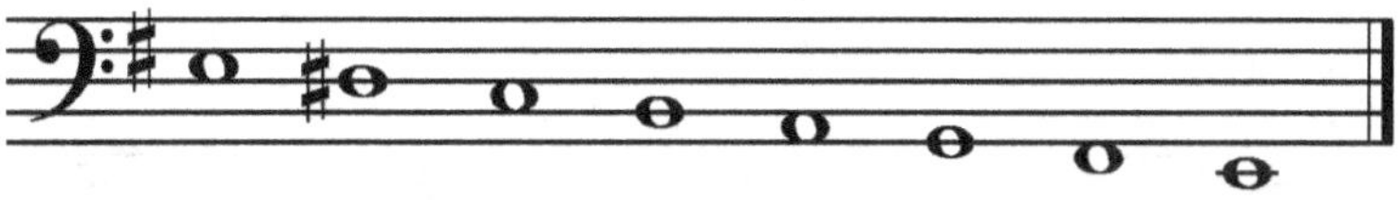

d) _____

e) _____

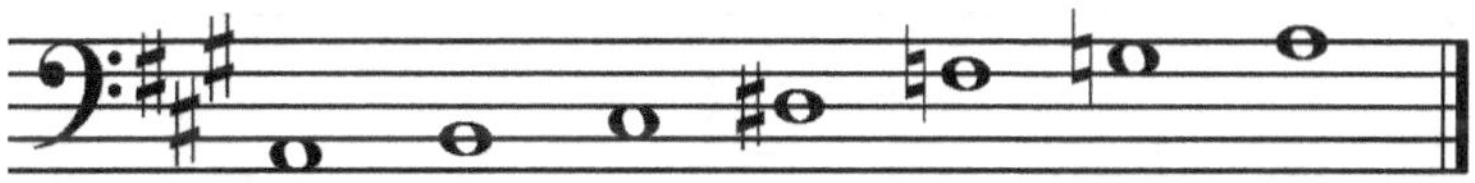

f) _____

g) _____

h) _____

i) _____

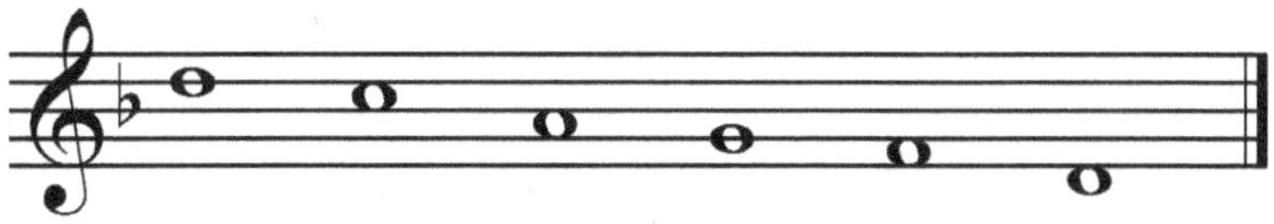

j) _____

# ULTIMATE MUSIC THEORY
## INTERMEDIATE EXAM SET #2 - EXAM #1

> ♪ **UMT Tip:** A Perfect Cadence and a Plagal Cadence both end on the Tonic. An Imperfect Cadence ends on the Dominant. Identify the key by identifying if the final bass note is the Tonic or Dominant in the Major key or in the relative minor key.

5. For each of the following cadences, name:
   a) the key.
   b) the type of cadence (Perfect, Plagal or Imperfect).

10

Key: _____   _____   _____

Type: _____   _____   _____

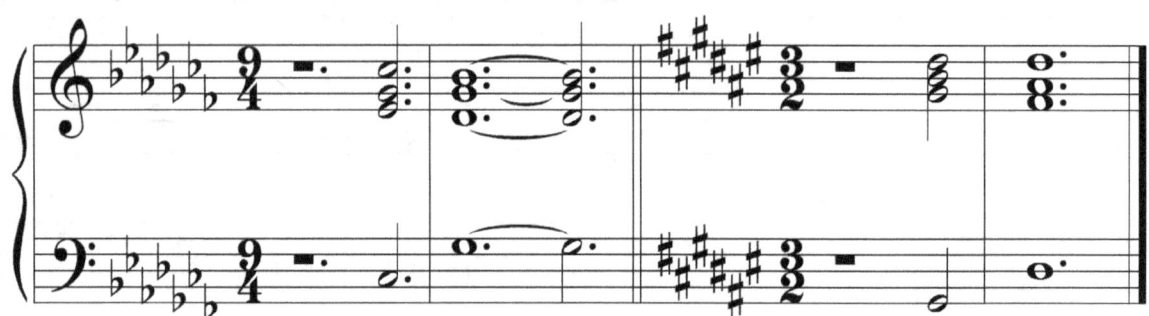

Key: _____                   _____

Type: _____                  _____

# ULTIMATE MUSIC THEORY
## INTERMEDIATE EXAM SET #2 - EXAM #1

> ♪ **UMT Tip:** Melodic fragments do not always start or end on the Tonic note. Look for accidentals which may indicate the raised 7th of a minor key.

6. For each of the following excerpts:
   a) Name the key.
   b) Add the correct Time Signature below the bracket.

__10__

Key: _____

Key: _____

Key: _____

Key: _____

Key: _____

UltimateMusicTheory.com © Copyright 2013 Gloryland Publishing. All Rights Reserved.

# ULTIMATE MUSIC THEORY
## INTERMEDIATE EXAM SET #2 - EXAM #1

♪ **UMT Tip:** Irregular groups are played in the time of a regular group of the same note value.
In Simple Time, 3 = 2, and 5, 6 or 7 = 4.
In Compound Time, 2 = 3, 4 = 3 and 5 or 7 = 3 or 6.

7. Add rests below each bracket to complete each measure.

# ULTIMATE MUSIC THEORY
## INTERMEDIATE EXAM SET #2 - EXAM #1

> ♪ **UMT Tip:** Use the Circle of Fifths to identify the Key Signature.

8. a) Name the following notes.

    ___
    10

    The Submediant of C Major is _____.

    The Tonic of F sharp Major is _____.

    The Subdominant of c sharp minor harmonic is _____.

    The Leading note of f minor harmonic is _____.

    The Supertonic of c minor is _____.

    b) For each of the following, name the Major key. Identify the technical degree name of the note.

    Major key: _____  _____  _____

    Technical
    degree name: _____  _____  _____

    Major key: _____  _____

    Technical
    degree name: _____  _____

UltimateMusicTheory.com © Copyright 2013 Gloryland Publishing. All Rights Reserved.

# ULTIMATE MUSIC THEORY
## INTERMEDIATE EXAM SET #2 - EXAM #1

> ♪ **UMT Tip:** Read the instructions carefully. Identify each Term and then match it to the correct definition.

9. Match each English definition with its Italian term. (Not all terms will be used.)

$\frac{\phantom{00}}{10}$

| Definition | | Term | |
|---|---|---|---|
| Maelzel's metronome | _____ | a) | *e* |
| brilliant | _____ | b) | *alla* |
| almost, as if | _____ | c) | *M.M.* |
| with movement | _____ | d) | *non* |
| and | _____ | e) | *poco a poco* |
| more | _____ | f) | *rubato* |
| not | _____ | g) | *brillante* |
| in the manner of | _____ | h) | *quasi* |
| little by little | _____ | i) | *con moto* |
| with some freedom of tempo to enhance musical expression | _____ | j) | *più* |
| | | k) | *animato* |

# ULTIMATE MUSIC THEORY
## INTERMEDIATE EXAM SET #2 - EXAM #1

> ♪ **UMT Tip:** The Time Signature is written in both the Treble Clef and the Bass Clef.

10. Analyze the following excerpt by answering the questions below.

## German Dance

*Allegretto*

Ludwig van Beethoven

a) Name the key of this piece. _____

b) Explain the tempo of this piece. _____

c) Add the Time Signature directly on the music.

d) Add the missing rest at the letter **A**.

e) For the triad at **B**, name: Root: ____ Type/Quality: _____ Position: _____

f) Explain the sign at the letter **C**. _____

g) Name the intervals at the following letters: **D** _____ **E** _____

h) Explain the sign at the letter **F**. _____

i) Identify the cadence at **G** as Perfect, Imperfect or Plagal. _____

j) Explain the sign at the letter **H**. _____

UltimateMusicTheory.com © Copyright 2013 Gloryland Publishing. All Rights Reserved.

# ULTIMATE MUSIC THEORY
## INTERMEDIATE EXAM SET #2 - EXAM #2

Total Score: ___
100

1. a) Write the following harmonic intervals above each of the given notes. Use whole notes.

    Major 7    diminished 5    Perfect 8    minor 7    Augmented 6

b) Invert the above harmonic intervals in the same clef. Name the inversions.

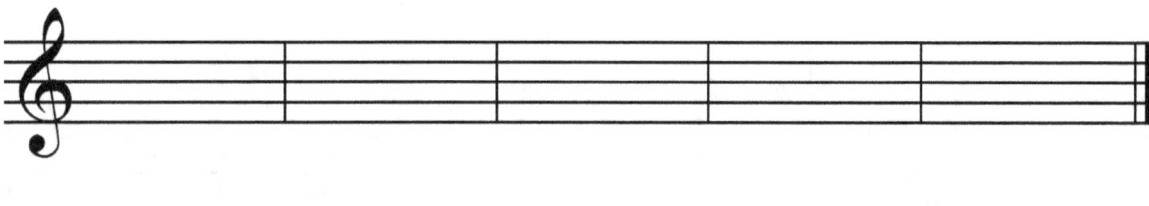

_____    _____    _____    _____    _____

c) Identify the following melodic intervals.

_____    _____    _____    _____    _____

d) Invert the above melodic intervals in the same clef. Name the inversions.

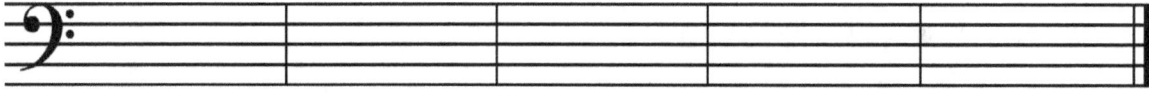

_____    _____    _____    _____    _____

UltimateMusicTheory.com © Copyright 2013 Gloryland Publishing. All Rights Reserved.

# ULTIMATE MUSIC THEORY
## INTERMEDIATE EXAM SET #2 - EXAM #2

2. a) Write the following Key Signatures in the Bass Clef.

__10__

The minor key with A as the Supertonic.

The Major key with D♯ as the Mediant.

The minor key with C as the Tonic.

The Major key with B as the Leading note.

The minor key with F♯ as the Dominant.

b) Name the following notes.

The Supertonic of f sharp minor harmonic.  _____

The Subdominant of e flat minor melodic.  _____

The Leading note of G flat Major.  _____

The Mediant of B flat Major.  _____

The Submediant of d minor melodic.  _____

UltimateMusicTheory.com © Copyright 2013 Gloryland Publishing. All Rights Reserved.

# ULTIMATE MUSIC THEORY
## INTERMEDIATE EXAM SET #2 - EXAM #2

3. The following melody is in the key of E Major.
   a) Transpose the given melody UP a minor third. Use the correct Key Signature. Name the key of the new melody.
   b) Transpose the given melody UP a diminished fifth. Use the correct Key Signature. Name the key of the new melody.

$\overline{10}$

Key: E Major

Key: _____

Key: _____

# ULTIMATE MUSIC THEORY
## INTERMEDIATE EXAM SET #2 - EXAM #2

4. Write the following scales, ascending and descending, in the given clefs. Use whole notes.

   a) The enharmonic Tonic Major scale of d sharp minor. Use accidentals.

   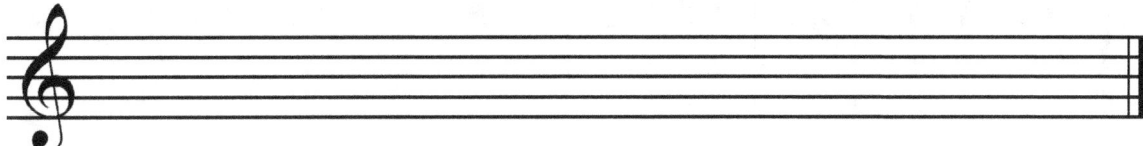

   b) The Tonic minor scale, harmonic form, of A flat Major. Use a Key Signature.

   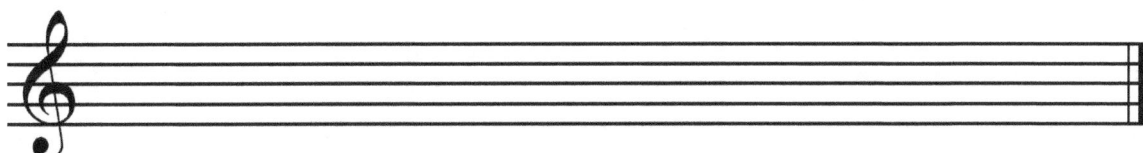

   c) The enharmonic relative minor scale, melodic form, of B Major. Use accidentals.

   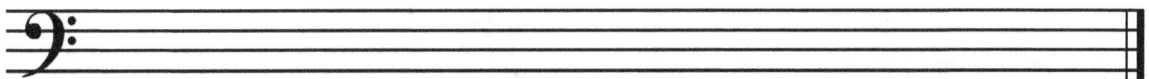

   d) Whole Tone scale beginning on G. Use accidentals. Use any standard notation.

   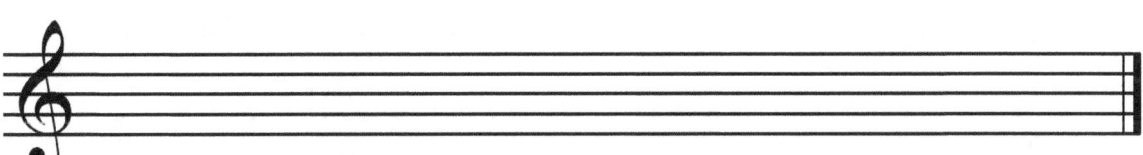

   e) Chromatic scale beginning on C. Use accidentals. Use any standard notation.

   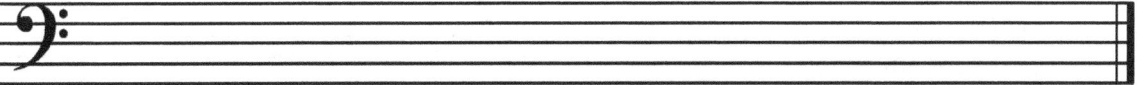

# ULTIMATE MUSIC THEORY
## INTERMEDIATE EXAM SET #2 - EXAM #2

5. For each of the following cadences, name:
   a) the key.
   b) the type of cadence (Perfect, Plagal or Imperfect).

Key: _____   _____   _____

Type: _____   _____   _____

c) Write the following triads in solid form in close position. Use whole notes. Use a Key Signature.

The Subdominant triad
of f minor harmonic
in second inversion.

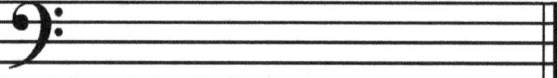

The Supertonic triad
of A Major
in root position.

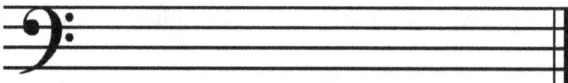

The Dominant triad
of c sharp minor harmonic
in first inversion.

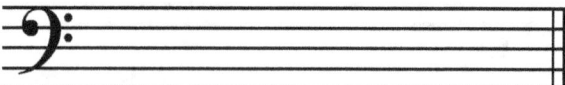

The Tonic triad
of D flat Major
in second inversion.

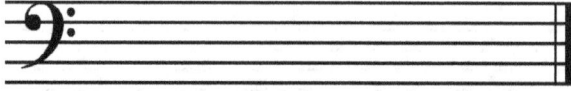

UltimateMusicTheory.com © Copyright 2013 Gloryland Publishing. All Rights Reserved.

# ULTIMATE MUSIC THEORY
## INTERMEDIATE EXAM SET #2 - EXAM #2

6. For each of the following excerpts:
   a) Name the key.
   b) Add the correct Time Signature below the bracket.

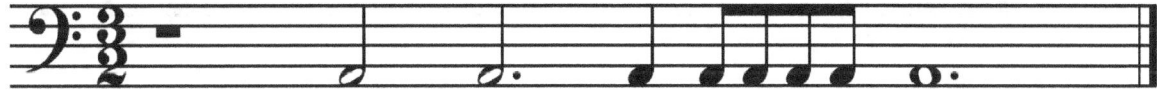

Key: _____

Key: _____

Key: _____

c) For each of the following excerpts, add bar lines.

7. Add rests below each bracket to complete each measure.

___
10

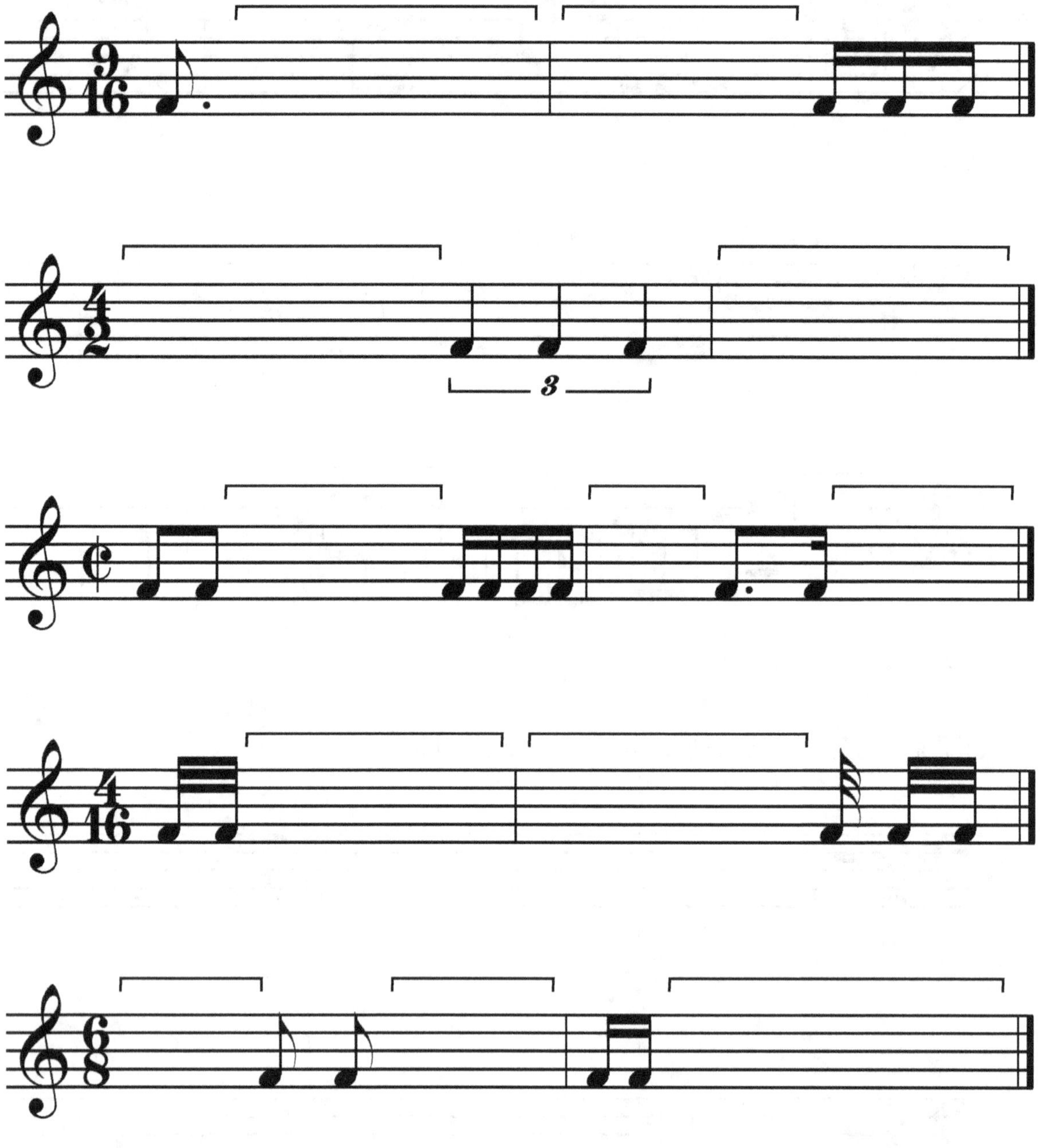

# ULTIMATE MUSIC THEORY
## INTERMEDIATE EXAM SET #2 - EXAM #2

8. a) Name the following scales as blues, chromatic, Major pentatonic, minor pentatonic, octatonic or whole tone.

10 _____

_____

_____

_____

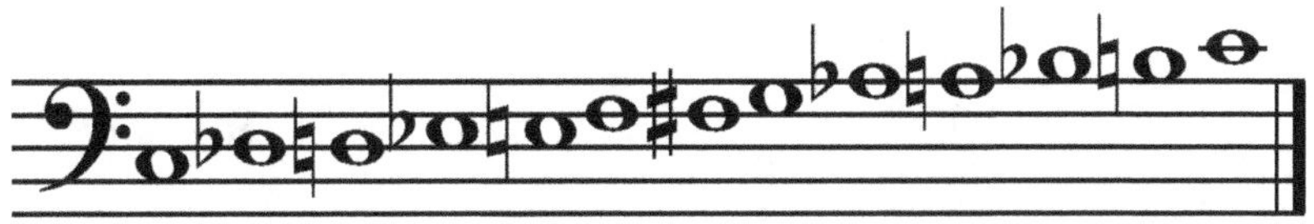

_____

_____

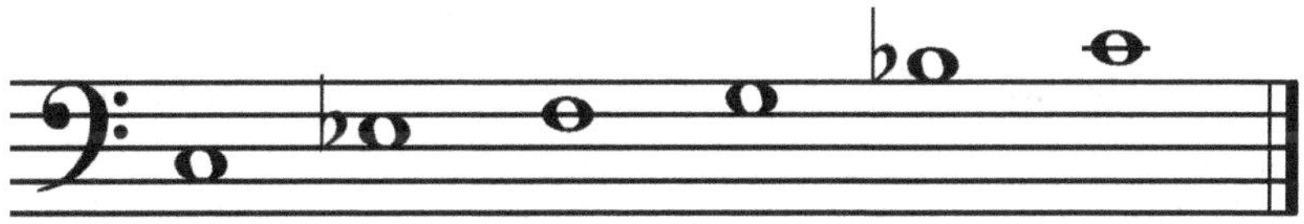

b) Identify the root note and the quality/type of each of the following triads.

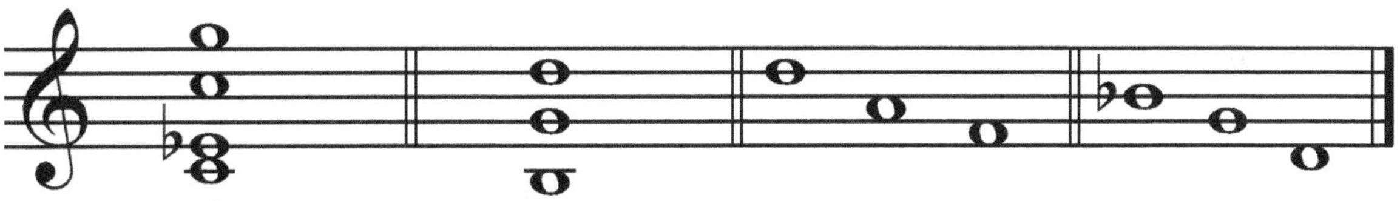

Root Note: _____  _____  _____  _____

Quality/Type: _____  _____  _____  _____

UltimateMusicTheory.com © Copyright 2013 Gloryland Publishing. All Rights Reserved.

# ULTIMATE MUSIC THEORY
## INTERMEDIATE EXAM SET #2 - EXAM #2

9. Match each musical term with its English definition. (Not all definitions will be used.)

<u>   </u>
10

| Term | | Definition |
|---|---|---|
| | | a) and |
| *spiritoso* | _____ | b) in the manner of |
| *accelerando* | _____ | c) quiet, tranquil |
| *all'* | _____ | d) more |
| *tranquillo* | _____ | e) spirited |
| *vivace* | _____ | f) too much |
| *troppo* | _____ | g) slow and solemn |
| *più* | _____ | h) without |
| *e* | _____ | i) becoming quicker |
| *fortepiano* | _____ | j) brilliant |
| *grave* | _____ | k) loud then suddenly soft |
| | | l) lively, brisk |

# ULTIMATE MUSIC THEORY
## INTERMEDIATE EXAM SET #2 - EXAM #2

10. Analyze the following excerpt by answering the questions below.

### Tricks, not Treats

*Grave*  
S. McKibbon

a) Name the title of this piece. _____

b) Explain the tempo of this piece. _____

c) Add the Time Signature directly on the music.

d) Name the notes at the letters: **A** _____  **B** _____

e) Name the notes at the letters: **C** _____  **D** _____

f) Name the notes at the letters: **E** _____  **F** _____

g) Circle an enharmonic equivalent in this piece. Label it as e.e.

h) Circle a diatonic semitone in this piece. Label it as d.s.

i) Circle a whole tone in this piece. Label it as w.t.

j) How many measures are in this piece? _____

UltimateMusicTheory.com © Copyright 2013 Gloryland Publishing. All Rights Reserved.

# ULTIMATE MUSIC THEORY
## INTERMEDIATE EXAM SET #2 - EXAM #3

Total Score: ____ / 100

1. a) Write the following melodic intervals above each of the given notes. Use half notes.

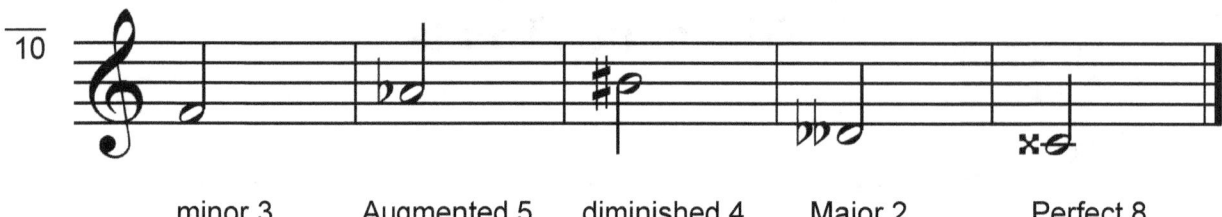

      minor 3    Augmented 5    diminished 4    Major 2    Perfect 8

b) Invert the above melodic intervals in the same clef. Use half notes. Name the inversions.

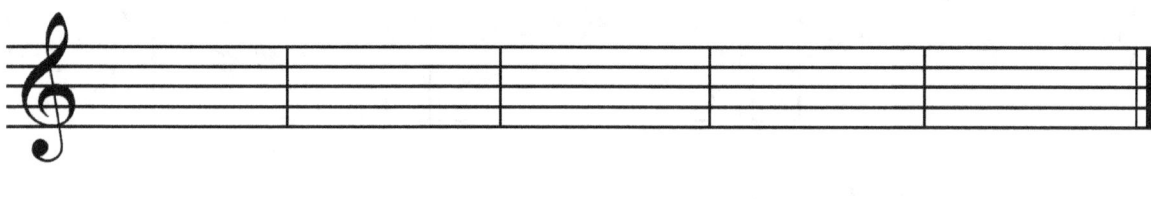

_____  _____  _____  _____  _____

c) Identify the following harmonic intervals.

_____  _____  _____  _____  _____

d) Invert the above harmonic intervals in the same clef. Use half notes. Name the inversions.

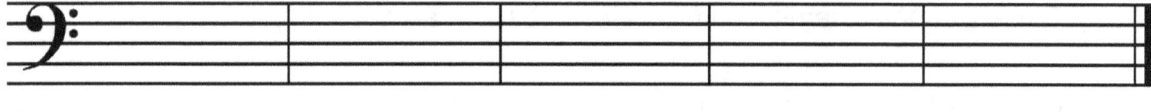

_____  _____  _____  _____  _____

UltimateMusicTheory.com © Copyright 2013 Gloryland Publishing. All Rights Reserved.

# ULTIMATE MUSIC THEORY
## INTERMEDIATE EXAM SET #2 - EXAM #3

2. a) Write the following triads in the Bass Clef. Use a Key Signature. Use solid form in close position. Use whole notes.

___
10

The Subdominant triad of
c sharp minor harmonic
in first inversion.

The Submediant triad of
E flat Major
in root position.

The Supertonic triad of
D flat Major
in second inversion.

The Dominant triad of
f minor harmonic
in root position.

The Mediant triad of
A Major
in first inversion.

b) Name the following notes.

The Submediant of C flat Major.  _____

The Subdominant of f sharp minor harmonic.  _____

The Leading note of a minor harmonic.  _____

The Supertonic of B flat Major.  _____

The Mediant of d minor harmonic.  _____

UltimateMusicTheory.com © Copyright 2013 Gloryland Publishing. All Rights Reserved.

# ULTIMATE MUSIC THEORY
## INTERMEDIATE EXAM SET #2 - EXAM #3

3. The following melody is in the key of F Major.
   a) Transpose the given melody UP a minor third. Use the correct Key Signature. Name the key of the new melody.
   b) Transpose the given melody UP an Augmented fourth. Use the correct Key Signature. Name the key of the new melody.

$\overline{10}$

Key: F Major

Key: _____

Key: _____

# ULTIMATE MUSIC THEORY
## INTERMEDIATE EXAM SET #2 - EXAM #3

4. Write the following scales, ascending and descending, in the given clefs. Use whole notes.

$\overline{10}$ a) The b flat minor scale, natural form. Use accidentals.

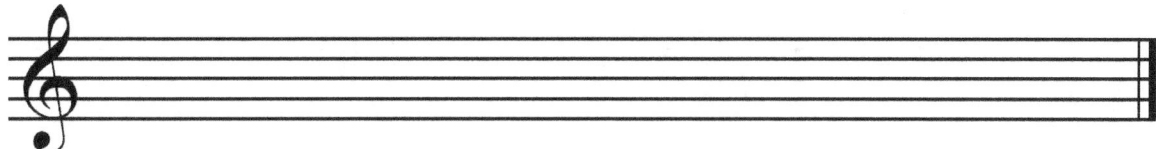

b) The Tonic minor scale, harmonic form, of C Major. Use a Key Signature.

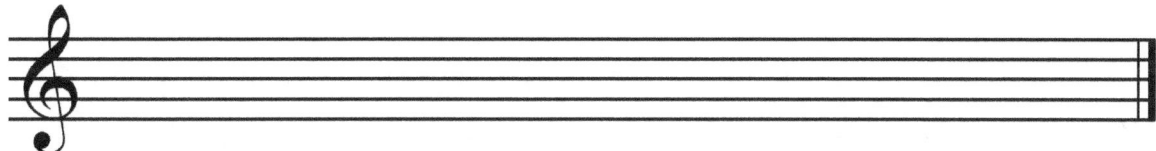

c) The relative minor scale, melodic form, of F sharp Major. Use accidentals.

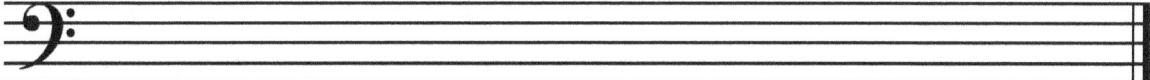

d) Whole Tone scale beginning on B. Use accidentals. Use any standard notation.

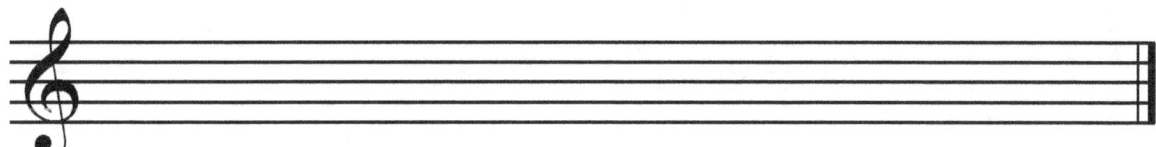

e) Chromatic scale beginning on F. Use accidentals. Use any standard notation.

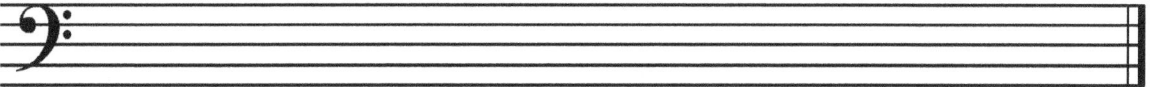

# ULTIMATE MUSIC THEORY
## INTERMEDIATE EXAM SET #2 - EXAM #3

5. For each of the following cadences, name:
   a) the key.
   b) the type of cadence (Perfect, Plagal or Imperfect).

___
10

Key: _____  _____  _____

Type: _____  _____  _____

Key: _____  _____

Type: _____  _____

# ULTIMATE MUSIC THEORY
## INTERMEDIATE EXAM SET #2 - EXAM #3

6. a) Add the correct Time Signature below the bracket.

b) For each of the following excerpts, add bar lines.

# ULTIMATE MUSIC THEORY
## INTERMEDIATE EXAM SET #2 - EXAM #3

7. Add rests below each bracket to complete each measure.

# ULTIMATE MUSIC THEORY
## INTERMEDIATE EXAM SET #2 - EXAM #3

8. a) Name the following scales as blues, chromatic, Major pentatonic, minor pentatonic, octatonic or whole tone.

   10

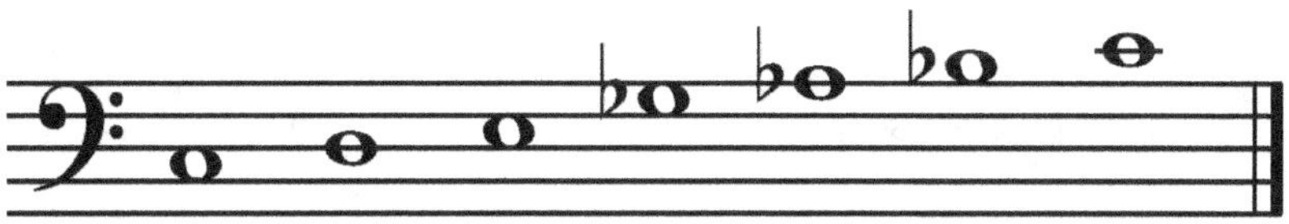

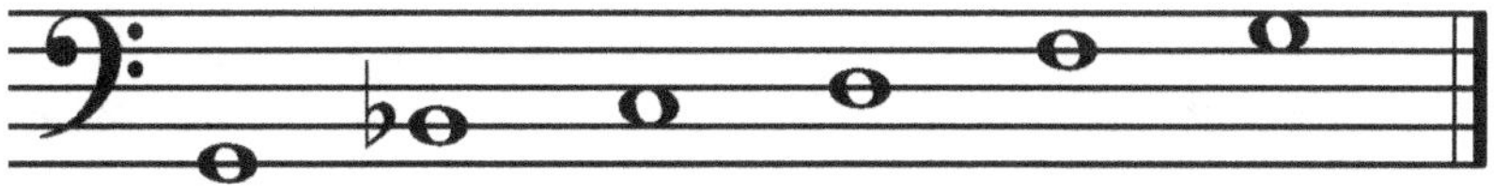

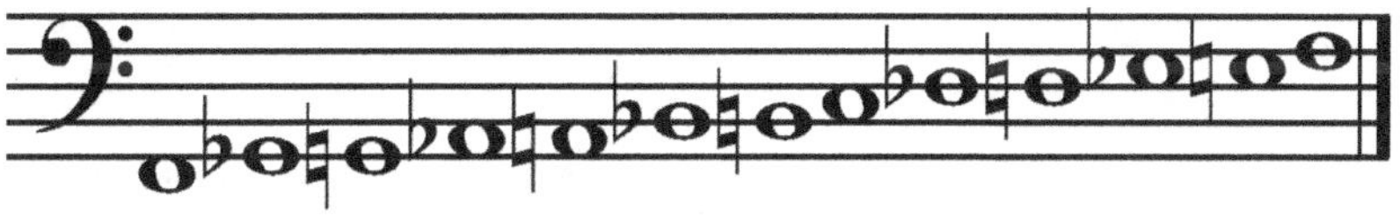

   b) Identify the root note and the quality/type of each of the following triads.

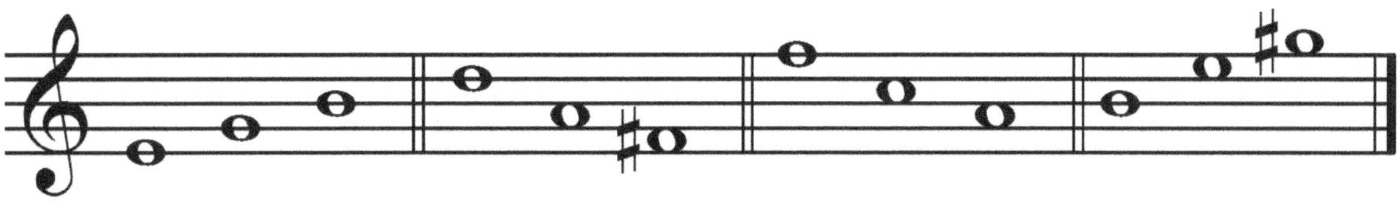

Root Note: _____  _____  _____  _____

Quality/Type: _____  _____  _____  _____

# ULTIMATE MUSIC THEORY
## INTERMEDIATE EXAM SET #2 - EXAM #3

9. Match each musical term with its English definition.  (Not all definitions will be used.)

$\dfrac{\phantom{10}}{10}$

| Term | | Definition |
|---|---|---|
| | | a) one string; depress the left piano pedal |
| spiritoso | _____ | b) with movement |
| meno mosso | _____ | c) light, nimble, quick |
| con moto | _____ | d) sweet, gentle |
| tre corde | _____ | e) not as slow as largo |
| larghetto | _____ | f) quiet, tranquil |
| leggiero | _____ | g) spirited |
| tranquillo | _____ | h) as fast as possible |
| dolce | _____ | i) less movement, slower |
| una corda | _____ | j) fast |
| presto | _____ | k) very fast |
| | | l) three strings; release the left piano pedal |

# ULTIMATE MUSIC THEORY
## INTERMEDIATE EXAM SET #2 - EXAM #3

10. Analyze the following piece by answering the questions below.

### Liam Drops his Spoon

*Allegretto*                                                                 S. McKibbon

a) Name the key of this piece. _____

b) Add the Time Signature directly on the music.

c) Name the scale at the letter **A**. _____

d) Name the intervals at the letters: **B** _____ **C** _____

e) Name the cadence at the letter **D**. _____

f) Explain the sign at the letter **E**. _____

g) Explain the sign at the letter **F**. _____

h) Name the cadence at the letter **G**. _____

i) How many measures are in this piece? _____

j) When performed, how many measures are played? _____

UltimateMusicTheory.com © Copyright 2013 Gloryland Publishing. All Rights Reserved.

# ULTIMATE MUSIC THEORY
## INTERMEDIATE EXAM SET #2 - EXAM #4

Total Score: ____
/100

1. a) Write the following melodic intervals above each of the given notes. Use half notes.

     diminished 5     Perfect 8     Augmented 4     minor 3     minor 7

b) Invert the above melodic intervals in the same clef. Use half notes. Name the inversions.

_____  _____  _____  _____  _____

c) Identify the following harmonic intervals.

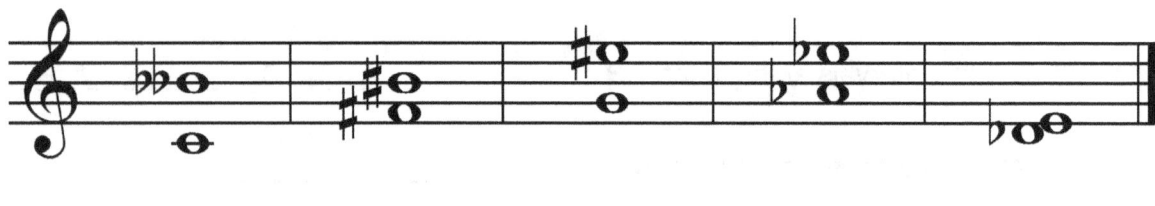

_____  _____  _____  _____  _____

d) Invert the above harmonic intervals in the same clef. Use whole notes. Name the inversions.

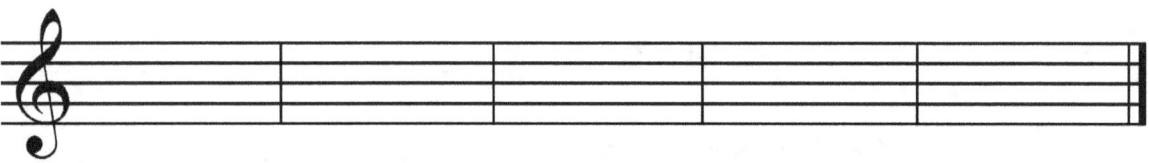

_____  _____  _____  _____  _____

UltimateMusicTheory.com © Copyright 2013 Gloryland Publishing. All Rights Reserved.

# ULTIMATE MUSIC THEORY
## INTERMEDIATE EXAM SET #2 - EXAM #4

2.  a) Write the following triads in the Bass Clef.  Use accidentals.  Use solid form in close position.  Use whole notes.

10

   The Tonic triad of
   c sharp minor harmonic
   in first inversion.

   The Mediant triad of
   E Major
   in root position.

   The Submediant triad of
   D Major
   in second inversion.

   The Dominant triad of
   d minor harmonic
   in first inversion.

   The Subdominant triad of
   B Major
   in root position.

   b) Name the following notes.

   The Leading Note of C flat Major.                           _____

   The Submediant of c minor harmonic.                         _____

   The Supertonic of a sharp minor harmonic.                   _____

   The Subdominant of B flat Major.                            _____

   The Mediant of g minor harmonic.                            _____

# ULTIMATE MUSIC THEORY
## INTERMEDIATE EXAM SET #2 - EXAM #4

3. The following melody is in the key of B flat Major.
   a) Transpose the given melody UP a minor third. Use the correct Key Signature. Name the key of the new melody.
   b) Transpose the given melody UP a Major second. Use the correct Key Signature. Name the key of the new melody.

$\overline{\phantom{10}}$
10

Key: B flat Major

Key: _____

Key: _____

# ULTIMATE MUSIC THEORY
## INTERMEDIATE EXAM SET #2 - EXAM #4

4. Write the following scales, ascending and descending, in the given clefs. Use whole notes.

$\overline{10}$ a) The e flat minor scale, natural form. Use a Key Signature.

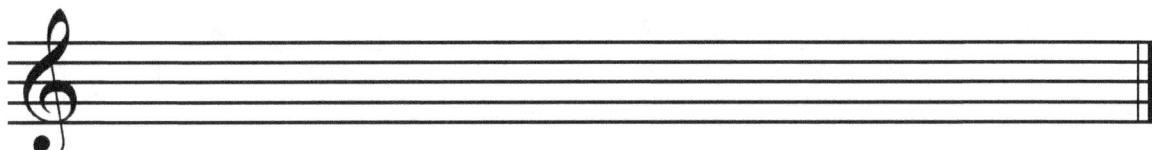

b) The Tonic minor scale, melodic form, of B flat Major. Use a Key Signature.

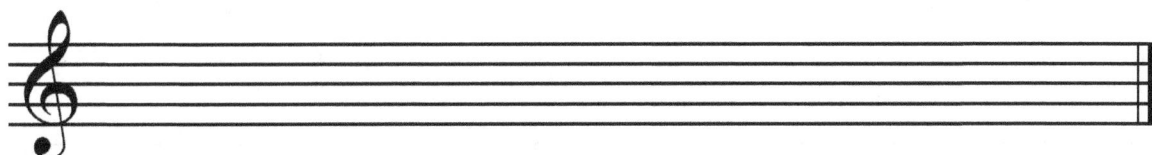

c) The relative minor scale, harmonic form, of B Major. Use accidentals.

d) Whole Tone scale beginning on G flat. Use accidentals. Use any standard notation.

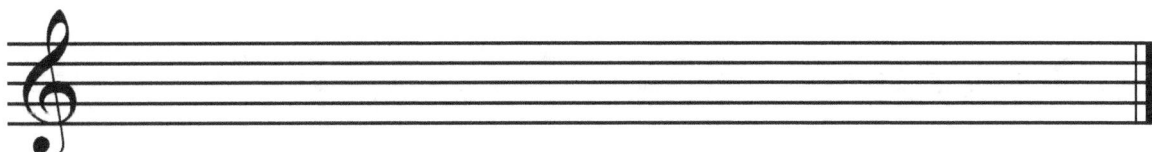

e) Chromatic scale beginning on C sharp. Use accidentals. Use any standard notation.

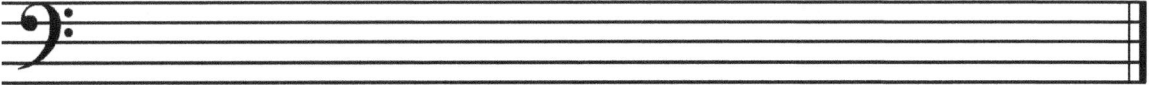

# ULTIMATE MUSIC THEORY
## INTERMEDIATE EXAM SET #2 - EXAM #4

5. For each of the following cadences, name:
   a) the key.
   b) the type of cadence (Perfect, Plagal or Imperfect).

___
10

Key: _____  _____  _____

Type: _____  _____  _____

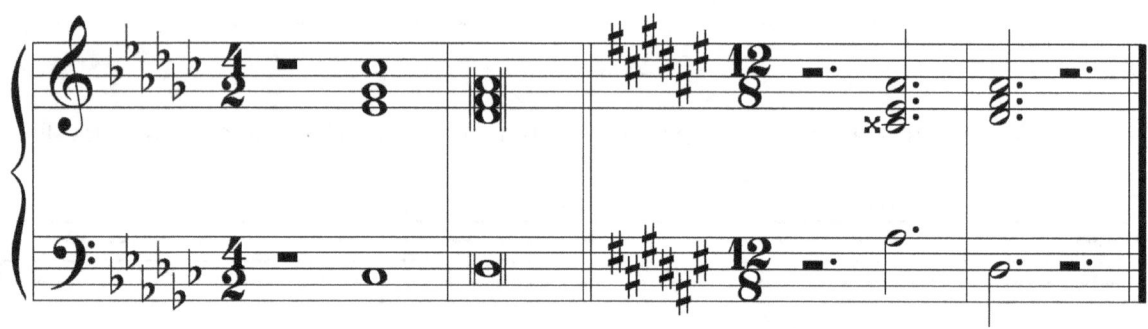

Key: _____  _____

Type: _____  _____

# ULTIMATE MUSIC THEORY
## INTERMEDIATE EXAM SET #2 - EXAM #4

6. a) Add the correct Time Signature below the bracket.

b) For each of the following excerpts, add bar lines.

# ULTIMATE MUSIC THEORY
## INTERMEDIATE EXAM SET #2 - EXAM #4

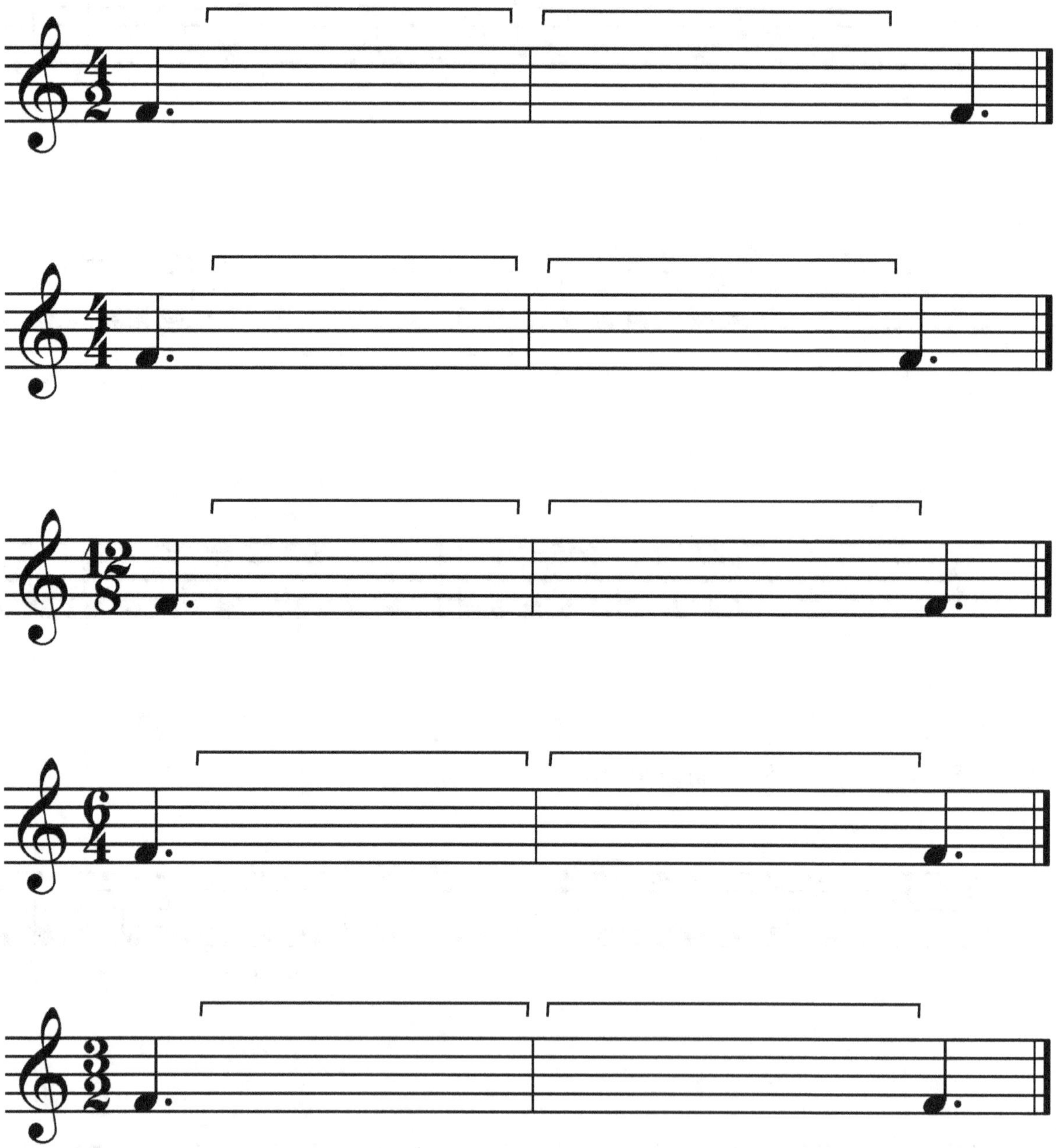

7. Add rests below each bracket to complete each measure.

# ULTIMATE MUSIC THEORY
## INTERMEDIATE EXAM SET #2 - EXAM #4

8. a) Name the following scales as blues, chromatic, Major pentatonic, minor pentatonic, octatonic or whole tone.

/10

b) Identify the root note and the quality/type of each of the following triads.

Root Note: _____   _____   _____   _____

Quality/Type: _____   _____   _____   _____

# ULTIMATE MUSIC THEORY
## INTERMEDIATE EXAM SET #2 - EXAM #4

9. Choose the Italian term which matches the definition on the left.

___
10

| Definition | Term Choices | | |
|---|---|---|---|
| Example: spirited | [X] spiritoso | [ ] espressivo | [ ] presto |
| much, very | [ ] ma | [ ] poco | [ ] molto |
| too much | [ ] senza | [ ] troppo | [ ] con moto |
| becoming quicker | [ ] accelerando | [ ] crescendo | [ ] diminuendo |
| loud, then suddenly soft | [ ] fortissimo | [ ] fortepiano | [ ] mezzo forte |
| held, sustained | [ ] tenuto | [ ] tie | [ ] staccato |
| always, continuously | [ ] quasi | [ ] rubato | [ ] sempre |
| quiet, tranquil | [ ] cantabile | [ ] tranquillo | [ ] leggiero |
| sweet, gentle | [ ] dolce | [ ] legato | [ ] maestoso |
| lively, brisk | [ ] presto | [ ] vivace | [ ] allegro |
| *Maelzel's metronome* | [ ] ed | [ ] M.M. | [ ] ma |

UltimateMusicTheory.com © Copyright 2013 Gloryland Publishing. All Rights Reserved.

# ULTIMATE MUSIC THEORY
## INTERMEDIATE EXAM SET #2 - EXAM #4

10. Analyze the following piece of music by answering the questions below.

## Owen Can Read!

**Animato**

S. McKibbon

a) Name the key of this piece. _____

b) Add the Time Signature directly on the music.

c) Name the scale at the letter **A**. _____

d) Name the intervals at the letters: **B** _____ **C** _____

e) At the triad at the letter **D**, name the Root: _____ Position: _____

f) Name the cadence at the letter **E**. _____

g) How many slurs are in this piece? _____

h) How many staccato notes are in this piece? _____

i) How many measures are in this piece? _____

j) When performed, how many measures are played? _____

 **Workbooks, Exams, Answers, Online Courses, App & More!**

A Proven Step-by-Step System to Learn Theory Faster - from Beginner to Advanced.

Innovative techniques designed to develop a complete understanding of music theory, to enhance sight reading, ear training, creativity, composition and musical expression.

## All UMT Series have matching Answer Books!

**The UMT Rudiments Series - Beginner A, Beginner B, Beginner C, Prep 1, Prep 2, Basic, Intermediate, Advanced & Complete (All-In-One)**

- ♪ 12 Lessons, Review Tests, and a Final Exam to develop confidence
- ♪ Music Theory Guide & Chart for fast and easy reference of theory concepts
- ♪ 80 Flashcards for fun drills to dramatically increase retention & comprehension

**Rudiments Exam Series - Preparatory, Basic, Intermediate & Advanced**

- ♪ 8 Exams plus UMT Tips on How to Score 100% on Theory Exams

## Each Rudiments Workbook correlates to a Supplemental Workbook.

**The UMT Supplemental Series - Prep Level, Level 1, Level 2, Level 3, Level 4, Level 5, Level 6, Level 7, Level 8 & Complete (All-In-One) Level**

- ♪ Form & Analysis and Music History - Composers, Eras & Musical Styles
- ♪ Melody Writing using ICE - Imagine, Compose & Explore
- ♪ 12 Lessons, Review Tests, Final Exam and 80 Flashcards for quick study

**Supplemental Exam Series - Level 5, Level 6, Level 7 & Level 8**

- ♪ 8 Exams to successfully prepare for nationally recognized Theory Exams

### UMT Online Courses, Music Theory App & More

- ♪ UMT Certification Course, Teachers Membership & Elite Educator Program
- ♪ Ultimate Music Theory App correlates to the Rudiments Workbooks
- ♪ Free Resources - Teachers Guide, Music Theory Blogs, videos & downloads

Go To: **UltimateMusicTheory.com**

www.ingramcontent.com/pod-product-compliance
Lightning Source LLC
Chambersburg PA
CBHW081735100526
44591CB00016B/2627